Standard
EASTER
PROGRAM
Book

Compiled by

Brynn Robertson

Standard
P U B L I S H I N G
Bringing The Word to Life™

Cincinnati, Ohio

Scripture quotations are taken from the HOLY BIBLE,
NEW INTERNATIONAL VERSION®. NIV®.
Copyright © 1973, 1978, 1984 by International Bible Society.
Used by permission of Zondervan. All rights reserved.

Standard Publishing Cincinnati, Ohio
A division of Standex International Corporation
© 2005 by Standard Publishing

ISBN 0-7847-1618-8

Contents

Praise
Dolores Steger

Praise is the sound that reaches the ear
In every Easter anthem we hear.
Praises for Jesus, for God's only Son.
Praises, He's risen; the victory's won.

Rolled Away
Dixie Phillips

One Savior died. *[hold up one finger]*
His disciples cried. *[rub eyes like crying]*
The stone was rolled away. *[roll hands]*
His disciples rejoiced that day!

It Really Happened
Cora M. Owen

It really happened that Christ arose
From a tomb one day.
Just at the break of early dawn,
God's power to display.

It really happened. He lives again,
And never will He die.
He lives forever. He's seated there
At God's throne up on high.

Why?

Dolores Steger

Why on a hilltop, against darkened sky,
There on a cross, why must Lord Jesus die?

Why? So in three days, against morning skies,
Jesus, as Savior of man, shall arise.

4-Given

Dixie Phillips

Three rusty nails! *[hold up three fingers with right hand]*
One rugged cross! *[hold up one finger with left hand]*
Forgiven people, *[hold up four fingers]*
Who once were lost.

Easter
Dolores Steger

Easter, oh, Easter, the wonder of spring,
So to You, God in Heaven, we pray
And thank You for Jesus, the Christ and the king,
The living Lord with us each day.

Show Me
Cora M. Owen

"Show me first, then I'll believe."
That's what some people say.
They have to see before there's faith.
This is their chosen way.

"Show me that Jesus is alive."
That is what Thomas said.
"Then I'll believe as He promised.
He's risen from the dead."

He has shown He is alive.
The Savior lives again.
It is recorded in God's Word.
By faith it covers our sin.

Oh, Joy!
Dolores Steger

Oh, joy, the tomb is empty!
Abandoned are the shrouds.
Our Lord and Savior's risen
To reign from Heaven's clouds.

He Tasted Death
Cora M. Owen

He tasted death that all might live.
Jesus, the Son of God,
By being punished in our stead,
A sacrifice unflawed.

He tasted death to live again.
Death could not hold Him fast.
Now He will live forevermore
With victory to last.

Can Say
Dixie Phillips

Little boys and girls can say,
"He has risen from the grave."
Little boys and girls can say,
"He's alive for me today!"

A Wonderful Story
Dolores Steger

It's a wonderful story; when did it begin?
With the death on the cross to wash away sin?

It's a wonderful story; it surely began
With one resurrected, the Son of Man.

Just Suppose He Didn't
Cora M. Owen

Just suppose Christ hadn't come
To bring salvation's gift,
Souls of humans to redeem,
Out of deep sin to lift.

Just suppose He didn't die
And shed His cleansing blood.
Blessed cross of Calvary,
Just like a rushing flood.

Just suppose He didn't rise
One morning out the tomb.
All would be forever dark,
And our hearts full of gloom.

Just suppose He won't come back
To claim His loved and own.
But praise His name! He will be here
To take us to His throne!

Love Is the Reason
Dolores Steger

Love is the reason that God sent His Son
To Golgotha to be crucified.
On a cross where, for man's sins, He suffered the slings
Of torment and painfully died.

Love is the reason that God in His grace
Worked a miracle there in a cave.
And had Jesus arise, walk on earth, be the way.
A Savior to mankind He gave.

Love is the reason, God's love for us all,
God's love, ever tender and dear.
A love, unrelenting through time and through space,
Love's the reason that Easter is here.

I Hold in My Hand

Kyle Wilson

I hold in my hand
Nothing
My life is not mine
For I'm the servant
Of the creator divine
He gives me what He sees fit
And takes away what He wants
He knew my life story
Before there was time
And on a rugged cross
The sinless Lamb was
Slaughtered
For those who were lost
He holds in His pierced
And bleeding hands
My life and yours
So nothing is what
I hold in my hand
For it is not mine
It belongs to the Lamb
And creator divine

Oh, What a Savior

Lenora McWhorter

Oh, what a Savior; oh, what a friend
That He'd give His life for evil men.

Oh, what suffering to be nailed to the cross.
Sent by the Father, so none would be lost.

Oh, what victory because He died.
He paid the debt when He was crucified.

WOW-MOM

Dixie Phillips

[Three children enter. Each carries a poster board with one letter on it. The first is M. The second is O. The third is M.]

FIRST M: *[holds up the M for audience to see]*
M is for the MILLION ways my mommy shows her love.
Some days I think she's an angel sent from Heaven above.

O: *[holds up the O for audience to see]*
O is the OUTSTANDING job my mommy always does
to show our family just how much we are loved.

SECOND M: *[holds up the M for audience to see]*
M is for the MAGNIFICENT ways she cares for me.
Without my precious mommy, I don't know where I'd be.

UNISON: *[All three turn their cards upside down and speak in unison.]*
There's only one word to describe the job our mommy does.
WOW! That's right, Mommy! You are number one.

The Bunny Tells the Meaning of Easter

John Cosper

Summary: The EASTER BUNNY tries to explain to a clueless guy the true story of Easter and of Jesus.

Characters:
NARRATOR
EASTER BUNNY—played by a girl
CHET—a guy who seems pretty clueless
Setting: the Easter Bunny's house
Props: door, an egg
Costumes: bunny costume

NARRATOR: This is a story about the Easter Bunny—that hippity-hoppity pal of children everywhere who delivers eggs and chocolate bunnies to good boys and girls around the world every year. Once upon a time, as Easter morning broke over the Western Hemisphere, the Easter Bunny had finished his rounds, and—

BUNNY: Whoa, 'scuse me—*his*? The Easter Bunny is a *her*.

NARRATOR: Oh, my apologies. I just assumed—

BUNNY: I know, you and your patriarchal view of the world assumed the Easter Bunny was a boy. Well, the Easter Bunny is a girl, so get it straight.

NARRATOR: My mistake. As I was saying, the bunny had finished hi—her rounds and was making her way back to her home on Bunny Trail.

BUNNY: Whoa, no giving away the Easter Bunny's secret, undisclosed home. That's what got the Easter Bunny into this mess in the first place.

NARRATOR: Indeed, it was. Because this year, a curious young man followed the Easter Bunny home.

[CHET enters and pounds on the door.]

CHET: Hey! Bunny, open up.

BUNNY: Sorry, the Easter Bunny doesn't live here.

CHET: So how come I saw the stupid bunny stop here?

BUNNY: Because . . . the Easter Bunny is a friend of the person who lives here . . . the Tooth Fairy.

CHET: The Tooth Fairy, huh? Well, open up. I need to talk to her too.

BUNNY: HIM! The Tooth Fairy is a him! Just because he's a fairy, you automatically assume—

CHET: Fine, whatever. Open up. I have a bone to pick with him.

BUNNY: A bone to pick or a tooth to pull?

[CHET kicks the door in.]

BUNNY: Hey! You're gonna pay for that!

CHET: So, you *are* the Easter Bunny.

BUNNY: What do you want?

CHET: I want an exchange of merchandise. *[holds up an egg]* You see this egg?

BUNNY: Yeah?

CHET: It's rotten.

BUNNY: You followed the Easter Bunny home over a stupid egg?

CHET: I certainly did.

BUNNY: You could have just gone to the store.

CHET: Hey, when I let a large, egg-distributing, talking rodent into my house, I expect quality.

BUNNY: Forgive the Easter Bunny for saying this, but the Easter Bunny thinks you're a nitwit.

CHET: Hey! You can't talk to me that way. You're supposed to bring joy and happiness to boys and girls like me.

BUNNY: Oh, my dear boy, surely you jest.

CHET: That is your job, isn't it?

BUNNY: Kid, the Easter Bunny brings eggs, true, and the Easter Bunny brings chocolate likenesses of the Easter Bunny. But joy and happiness . . . that's another fella's department—the one who is really behind the Easter celebration.

CHET: And who might that be?

BUNNY: Why Jesus, of course.

[CHET stares blankly.]

BUNNY: Jesus Christ? *[pauses]* The Son of God born at Christmastime to the virgin Mary? *[longer pause]* Kid, have a seat, and let the Easter Bunny enlighten you.

NARRATOR: And so the Easter Bunny began to relate the Easter story. Beginning with the separation of God and man in the Garden of Eden. The Easter Bunny explained that God loved the world so much, He gave His only Son as a sacrifice for the sins of the world, raising Him from the dead and opening the way for mankind to have eternal life.

CHET: I don't get it. If that's the meaning of Easter, where do *you* fit in?

BUNNY: The Easter Bunny is really nothing more than a holdover from the pagan celebration of the coming of spring. But in a way, the Easter Bunny's egg-delivery service and the resurrection fit together.

The Bunny Tells the Meaning of Easter

CHET: Oh yeah?

BUNNY: Spring is the time of the renewing of life. Eggs and the Easter Bunny are symbols of new life. On the other hand, Jesus is new life and eternal life for those who believe in Him.

NARRATOR: The young man considered all these things in his heart, pondering the meaning of the bunny's words. After a long pause, he finally spoke and asked . . .

CHET: How come you're talking about yourself in the third person?

BUNNY: How come the Easter Bunny is what? Have you not heard a word the Easter Bunny has said?

CHET: Yes, and you're still doing it.

BUNNY: The Easter Bunny is trying to get it into your thick skull that the true meaning of Easter is Jesus.

CHET: Yeah? Well, Jesus never promised me eggs and bunnies when I sat on His lap in the mall. *You* did. Now I want my eggs and I want them now!

BUNNY: You want eggs? *[smashes a raw egg on CHET's head]* You got 'em. *[hops away]*

NARRATOR: Suddenly the young man, quite confused, woke up from his dream.

CHET: *[rubs his eyes]* Wow! What was all *that* about? I almost forgot the true meaning of Easter.

NARRATOR: *[to audience]* We hope you remember the true meaning of Easter and remember the moral of the story: Find Easter's meaning in Jesus and not in the big bunny . . .

NARRATOR & CHET: . . . or else you'll get an egg that is runny.

The Bunny Tells the Meaning of Easter

The Facts of the Resurrection

Lenora McWhorter

Summary: A dramatic reading for youth using the letters of the word *resurrection* to make an acrostic.
Characters:
12 YOUTH
Props: 12 pieces of poster board with letters on each to spell out *resurrection*
Costumes: white robes are recommended

    R — Raised from the dead
    E — Early on the first day of the week
    S — Seen alive by many
    U — Unwrapped himself from the grave clothes
    R — Raised in power
    E — Reminded the disciples
    E — Eternally alive
    C — Completed His mission
    T — Took the stain of death
    I — Inside us with the Holy Spirit
    O — Omnipotent
    N — Never to die again

The Easter Present

John Cosper

Summary: A Sunday school teacher brings JESUS to class to show her students her favorite Easter gift.
Characters:
DENISE—girl around eight
SHANNON—girl around eight
BRIAN—boy around eight
ABBIE—girl around eight
MISS BROOKS—middle-aged woman, Sunday school teacher
JESUS—wearing white robe, scars in hands and feet
Setting: Sunday school classroom
Props: chairs, identical stuffed bunnies
Costumes: Sunday-best clothes for kids and teacher, Bible-times costume for JESUS

The stage is set like a Sunday school room. One chair is at the center. DENISE, dressed for Easter Sunday, enters carrying a stuffed bunny.

DENISE: Here we are, Mr. Bunny. What do you think? This is my Sunday school class. Aren't you so happy to be here? *[hugs the bunny]* Oh, I do love you so, Mr. Bunny! You're going to win first prize! Yes you are! 'Cause you're the cutest . . .

[SHANNON enters with an identical bunny. DENISE continues with her line. SHANNON finishes the line with her as she enters.]

DENISE & SHANNON: And cuddliest and prettiest bunny in the whole wide world!

[DENISE and SHANNON look at each other's bunnies.]

DENISE: Say, what's the big idea? How did you get a Mr. Bunny?
SHANNON: Because *I* was a good girl, and the Easter Bunny brought him to me.
DENISE: He . . . you . . . you can't have a Mr. Bunny too! Mr. Bunny's a special one-of-a-kind, and . . . and that means yours is a fake Mr. Bunny!
SHANNON: He is not!
DENISE: Is too! *I* have the real Mr. Bunny.

[ANNIE runs into the room with another identical bunny.]

ABBIE: Hey, guys, look what the Easter Bunny brought—*[sees the other bunnies]* me?

DENISE: Oh look, Shannon. Another fake Mr. Bunny.

[BRIAN enters with yet another identical bunny.]

BRIAN: Here we are, Mr. Bunny. Welcome to Sunday school!

ABBIE: Brian?

BRIAN: Hey, cool! You guys got Mr. Bunny too?

DENISE: I don't believe this! *[to her bunny]* Why didn't you tell me there was a bunch of you?

[MISS BROOKS enters.]

MISS BROOKS: Good morning, children.

SHANNON: Good morning, Miss Brooks.

MISS BROOKS: I see you all brought your Easter presents.

ABBIE: Yep! Just like you asked us to!

DENISE: 'Cept theirs are all fakes. I got the real Mr. Bunny.

SHANNON: Do not!

MISS BROOKS: All right, girls. Settle down.

[MISS BROOKS sits in the chair. The children sit on the floor in a semicircle: DENISE and SHANNON on MISS BROOKS's right, BRIAN AND ABBIE on her left.]

ABBIE: So which one of us wins the prize?

DENISE: Yeah, who's got the coolest Easter present? Me, right?

MISS BROOKS: I don't know. They're all pretty special.

BRIAN: *[impatient]* Come on, Miss Brooks! Who gets the candy?

ABBIE: Miss Brooks, what did the Easter Bunny bring you?

MISS BROOKS: I didn't get anything from the Easter Bunny.

SHANNON: But you said you were gonna show us your Easter present.

MISS BROOKS: I am, but my present didn't come from the Easter Bunny.

BRIAN: So what did you get?

MISS BROOKS: Here He comes now.

[JESUS enters, stands beside MISS BROOKS.]

DENISE: A boyfriend?

MISS BROOKS: No, Denise. This is my best friend in the world—Jesus.

BRIAN: Whoa. You're . . . you're Jesus?

[JESUS nods. The kids all ooh and aah over Him.]

ABBIE: Can I . . . uh, can I give Him a hug?
MISS BROOKS: Of course you may.

[ABBIE stands up. JESUS reaches out to her. The kids see the scar and gasp in horror. ABBIE steps back.]

ABBIES: Eww! *[to MISS BROOKS]* What happened to His hand?
MISS BROOKS: It was pierced by a nail. If you look, you'll see He has scars
   on His other hand and His feet.
DENISE: But why?
MISS BROOKS: Because of us.

[The kids perk up in horror, wondering what they did.]

SHANNON: Well, maybe you all did something, but it wasn't my fault!
ABBIE: Mine either!
DENISE: Me three! I deny everything!

[The girls look at BRIAN accusingly.]

BRIAN: What? I didn't do it either! *[to MISS BROOKS]* Did I?

MISS BROOKS: It wasn't any one thing you did, Brian. And it wasn't all because of you. It was because of Denise, Abbie, and Shannon. And me.

SHANNON: How come He got those marks because of us?

MISS BROOKS: Do you remember what we talked about last week?

DENISE: Sin!

MISS BROOKS: And do you remember what sin is?

DENISE: It was when Shannon pulled my hair.

BRIAN: And when I tried to teach my sister to fly by pushing her off the couch.

MISS BROOKS: Well, *[pauses]* does anybody remember our Bible verse from last week?

ABBIE: "For the wages of sin is death, but the gift of God is eternal life in Christ Jesus our Lord," Romans 6:23.

MISS BROOKS: What does that verse mean, Abbie?

ABBIE: It means all of us are sinners and deserve to die, but He made it so we didn't have to die because He loves us!

MISS BROOKS: That's right. God loves us so much, He sent His Son Jesus to die in our place.

DENISE: You mean He died for us?

BRIAN: That's how He got the scars?

MISS BROOKS: Exactly.

ABBIE: Wow.

SHANNON: So I guess that means we lose the contest, huh?

MISS BROOKS: No, we all got the best present.

BRIAN: You and me?

MISS BROOKS: All of us! Jesus gave us eternal life, and that present is for all of us!

SHANNON: Aww! We all get the best present!

DENISE: Yeah. Who needs a stupid bunny when you got Jesus? *[tosses the bunny over her shoulder]*

Through a Mother's Eyes
by Ruth Powell

Summary: A woman delivers a monologue that tells a story of Jesus from the perspective of what MARY may have seen as Jesus' mother.
Characters:
MARY—any age

Long ago—so long ago that you may forget—a baby boy was born. Just another little baby born in a temporary shelter in Bethlehem. His mother held Him against her heart and knew, as all mothers know, the joy and anguish of the first holding. This was her tiny, new son, defenseless and dependent upon her gentleness and love.

Shepherds came, filled with the wonder of angels' song, to bow before the newborn child. Later there were the strangers, those men from the East with their expensive gifts, suitable for a king—and a death—and a burial.

The child grew. He stood alone but reached His little hand to hold hers, and she held on tightly. For these brief years, He was hers. She sang to Him, played with Him, walked with Him about the little village and the quiet hills and tucked Him into bed each night with a prayer.

One day, with His eyes bright with tenderness only He possessed, He said, "You know, don't you, that I must be about my Father's business?" And she knew. She turned with Him toward home and smiled as she watched Him pick up a stick to trail in the dusty road. She watched Him stride ahead, tall and strong, His young hand firmly clasped around the stick which He lifted now and again into the air until at last He brought it to rest, lightly, on His shoulder.

Then suddenly her eyes grew dim with tears. She started to call Him to her side. It was in that moment, for one breathless instant, she had seen His image blur. It almost seemed that the stick He bore on His shoulder had taken on the shape of a cross.

Disbelief

John Cosper

Summary: A Pharisee's servant tells a fellow servant about Christ's death on the cross, wondering if He was the Messiah.
Characters:
ESTHER and MARTHA—servants of a Pharisee
Setting: the home of a member of the Jewish ruling council, the night Jesus was crucified
Props: Bible-times furniture and dishes
Costumes: Bible-times costumes of servants' robes

The scene takes place in the home of one of the members of the Jewish ruling council. ESTHER is drying some dishes as MARTHA enters. ESTHER pauses and looks up, then resumes drying.

ESTHER: Some storm out there.

MARTHA: Yes, it was.

ESTHER: Is He still out there?

MARTHA: No. He died right before the storm hit.

ESTHER: Ah.

MARTHA: It was bizarre, Esther. He cried out, His head fell, and then He was gone. One of the soldiers pierced His side to be sure, and the next thing we knew, there was the storm and an earthquake.

ESTHER: Interesting.

MARTHA: I heard one of the soldiers right after, saying, "Surely this man was the Son of God." It really made me wonder if the stories aren't true.

[There is a pause, as ESTHER doesn't reply.]

MARTHA: But then . . . if He was the Son of God, why would He allow mere men to kill Him like that?

ESTHER: Exactly my thought.

MARTHA: Listen to you. Just like the rest of the mob that was crying for His death today. You believed in Him once.

ESTHER: I . . . I didn't know what to believe.

MARTHA: You saw Him perform miracles. He healed the crippled, the blind—even raised the dead.

ESTHER: So we heard.

MARTHA: We witnessed Him healing the blind and lame with our own eyes, did we not?

ESTHER: Maybe so. But that does not make Him the Son of God.

MARTHA: You were the one who first believed. You convinced me that it might be possible. Why is it so hard to believe now?

ESTHER: Last night I was in the courtyard while our master met with the council. There were a good number of us out there, staying warm by the fire. And right in the middle of it was one of His followers.

MARTHA: Who?

ESTHER: I don't know his name. He was a fisherman, I believe, before he hooked up with Jesus. Every time I saw Jesus, he was right there next to Him. I thought if anyone could shed some light on what Jesus was doing with the council, he would. So I said to him, "You were with this man in the temple." He denied it, saying he never knew Jesus. One of the other servants there spoke up. "Yes, you were. I've seen you with Jesus before!" He denied it again, this time a little more aggressively. Once more we asked, "Were you not with Jesus? Haven't we seen you with Him?" He began to curse and scream, saying he never knew Him. Right about that time, a cock crowed. The man got this look of terror in his eyes . . . and then he saw Jesus, eye to eye. He ran out of the court and disappeared into the night.

MARTHA: And you're sure he was with Jesus?

ESTHER: I know that face. I've seen him so many times before. Maybe Jesus was a prophet or just a wise teacher. But if Jesus was really the Son of God, how come His own friends denied Him in His hour of trial?

The Café at Emmaus

John Cosper

Summary: A modern-day dramatization of the story of the two men walking to Emmaus who encounter the risen Christ (Luke 24:13-35).

Characters:

CLEOPAS and SIMON—2 believers

JESUS

ANNA—a hostess

HELEN—a waitress

Setting: café

Props: tables, chairs, menus, other restaurant furnishings, apron, tray of drinks, basket of bread, fake money

Costumes: modern-dress for all the characters, apron for HELEN

JESUS, CLEOPAS, and SIMON enter following ANNA. She leads them to a table, set for three, at center. She hands each of the men a menu.

CLEOPAS: So let me see if I have this: if Jesus was in fact the Messiah, then He was meant to suffer all the indignities of the past few days.

JESUS: Exactly.

SIMON: I would never have put that together myself. I've read the prophets dozens and dozens of times. Never caught that the lamb to the slaughter was supposed to be the Messiah.

[HELEN enters.]

CLEOPAS: Well, the religious leaders have always told us that the Messiah would be a conquering king who would deliver us from Rome.

SIMON: Can you imagine what it would mean if the religious leaders were responsible for the death of the Messiah? And if the report we heard about the empty tomb was true?

HELEN: Let me guess, we're discussing the king of the Jews.

CLEOPAS: Jesus? Yes, how did you know?

HELEN: Everybody who's passed through that door has mentioned it this weekend. Everyone's talked about the storm and the earthquake and the dead rising from the grave.

SIMON: Did you see any of it?

HELEN: No, hon, I was working. But I could tell it as if I were there. Give it a few weeks, and no one will even mention His name anymore.

CLEOPAS: I'm not so sure about that. According to our friend here, this may be only the beginning of something new.

HELEN: Is that so?

CLEOPAS: See, everyone's always assumed the Messiah would be a mighty king and ruler because the prophets described how great and powerful He was.

HELEN: I went to Vacation Torah School. I heard the prophecies.

CLEOPAS: But the prophets also talk about the Messiah suffering and dying like a sacrificial lamb.

HELEN: Sounds contradictory to me.

SIMON: Until you realize why He had to die. He was the perfect sacrifice for our sins. Until now, we've had to rely on the priests to atone for our sins with sacrificial lambs. But Jesus was without sin. He was the sacrificial lamb. And because He died, our sins can be forgiven completely. Now we can have eternal life.

CLEOPAS: And now that He has power over sin and death, Jesus has become the great ruler the prophets foretold.

HELEN: But He's dead himself, right?

SIMON: Well . . . supposedly some women went to His tomb this morning to finish burial preparations and . . .

HELEN: And His body was gone.

SIMON: You heard about that?

HELEN: The soldiers at the tomb stopped in for brunch. They said the body was stolen.

CLEOPAS: Stolen?

HELEN: That's what they said.

The Café at Emmaus

SIMON: Are you sure it was their words or the words of the Sanhedrin?

CLEOPAS: Yeah. And if it were stolen, wouldn't the soldiers be put to death for failing to do their duty?

HELEN: I don't know, guys. I'm only a waitress. Now how about if I start you off with some drinks and a basket of fresh bread?

CLEOPAS: Sounds great.

JESUS: Yes, thank you.

[HELEN exits.]

CLEOPAS: Well, it has certainly been educational meeting You. If everything You told us on the road is true, we were witnesses to the coming of the Messiah.

SIMON: And we may be witnesses to His resurrection.

CLEOPAS: Yeah, we definitely need to find out what happened this morning.

JESUS: I think you'll find that the testimony of the women was true.

SIMON: Are You sure about that?

JESUS: *[smiles knowingly]* Pretty sure.

[HELEN enters with a tray of drinks and basket of bread.]

HELEN: Here you go, fellas. Need another moment with the menus?

CLEOPAS: Please.

[HELEN exits.]

JESUS: I want to thank you again for inviting me to break bread with you.

CLEOPAS: We should be thanking You for sharing Your insights with us today.

SIMON: Yes, thank You. It's been a real eye-opener.

JESUS: *[smiles]* Shall I bless the food?

CLEOPAS: Please do.

[JESUS picks up a piece of bread and breaks it. A quick flash of light and then the lights go black for a few seconds. The lights come back up and CLEOPAS and SIMON stand beside JESUS' empty chair, gawking.]

CLEOPAS: Did you just . . . Did He just . . . Did we just see—?

[HELEN enters.]

HELEN: What happened to your friend? Tired of the Messiah talk?

SIMON: It was He!

HELEN: Who?

CLEOPAS: *[fumbling for words]* It was . . . it was the Christ!

SIMON: The Messiah!

CLEOPAS: Jesus!

HELEN: Are you sure?

CLEOPAS: Very sure! It was He!

SIMON: Weren't our hearts burning while He talked with us on the road and opened the Scriptures to us?

CLEOPAS: He has risen from the dead! Just like He said!

SIMON: We have to tell the others! Come on!

[They start to run off while HELEN remains.]

HELEN: What about dinner?

[CLEOPAS throws some money on the table.]

CLEOPAS: No time. We have to go spread the news that Jesus is alive!

[HELEN picks up the broken pieces of bread.]

HELEN: Hey, guys, wait for me!

[HELEN takes off her apron and runs after them.]

Famous Last Words

John Cosper

Summary: A journalist is assigned to discover the meaning in JESUS' last words, "It is finished," and sets out to interview people who knew JESUS.
Characters:
MARY MAGDALENE—devoted follower of Christ. She is dressed in black, in mourning for Christ's death.
JESUS—dressed in white
NEWSREEL—news announcer with an annoying, radio personality voice
MARCUS—news producer, a busy man in dress slacks, white shirt, and loosened tie
ESTHER—an elderly Jewish woman
ZECHARIAS—priest, dressed formally in priestly attire
DANIEL—a teenage boy, dressed in designer fashions
JUNA—a young girl full of life, dressed very cute
BARABBAS—a tough guy, dressed in leather jacket and boots, very rugged
Setting: various locations in ancient Israel
Props: cell phone, a video screen, the stone in the garden
Costumes: modern dress for all the characters. The goal is to make these Bible figures identifiable to today's audience and aid the audience in relating to their stories.

This play opens in a spoof of Citizen Kane, *with a NEWSREEL chronicling the life and death of JESUS. This sets up the news producer's desire to discover the meaning behind Jesus' last words, "It is finished." The NEWSREEL can be a video, as elaborate or simple as you can produce or an audio recording if that makes things simpler. You may also choose to perform it live with one or both actors trading off lines throughout the newscast.*

The stage lights are dim. MARY MAGDALENE is onstage, kneeling. She is outside the tomb of JESUS, crying. JESUS approaches her from stage right.

JESUS: Woman, why are you crying?
MARY: They have taken my Lord away, and I don't know where they have put Him.
JESUS: Who is it you are looking for?
MARY: *[turns to look at JESUS]* Sir, if you have carried Him away, tell me where You have put Him, and I will get Him.

[Lights fade down.]

NEWSREEL: *[voice heard from offstage]* And now, news from around the empire!!! The voice of the Roman Empire, spreading news from Asia to Gaul about our great Caesar and the empire forged by the Roman nation. Dateline: Jerusalem. To some, He was a hero. To others, a traitor. And still others claimed He was the Son of the Jewish God. Today the body of Jesus Christ lies interred in a hillside grave. The mystic carpenter from Nazareth who entertained many with His miracles and infuriated many more with His religious speech, died Friday by crucifixion by order of Governor Pontius Pilate. For three years Jesus made headlines throughout the territory. But His story goes back much further than that. At His birth in the tiny town of Bethlehem, a brilliant star shone brightly on the stable where He lay. That first night, JESUS received a visit from shepherds who claimed they heard angels announcing the birth of the one the Hebrews called the Messiah. At age 12, He confounded scholars with His knowledge of the Hebrew Scripture during a visit to the temple at Jerusalem. Twenty years later, He performed His first miracle, transforming water into wine at a wedding at Cana in Galilee. Then while preaching to a mountainside full of people, He took a basketful of bread and fish and fed more than 5,000 men! He healed the sick, blind, and lame. His miraculous hand touched Jew, Samaritan, and even Romans. It was even rumored that Jesus could raise the dead back to life. Many people left everything behind to follow Jesus. They hailed Him as the Messiah, the king written of by ancient prophets who would deliver the Israelites from slavery.

[MARCUS enters, listening to the last of the NEWSREEL.]

NEWSREEL: Yet in spite of all the hope He brought to the people of Judea, His heavy-handed preaching of submission and sacrifice made Him many enemies. Ultimately the Jewish religious leaders arrested Jesus and surrendered Him to the Roman authorities, demanding His execution for breaking their religious law. Some say He was innocent, having committed no crime. Others say He was a threat to Caesar himself. Whatever Jesus might have been, He is now dead and buried within the family tomb of one of His disciples, ironically a member of the Jewish religious council.

[NEWSREEL ends. MARCUS pulls out a cell phone.]

MARCUS: Leo, it's Marcus. I just finished listening to the Newsreel about Jesus. Great stuff here, but the ending is a little abrupt. We need a coda—a big finish to make this story complete, and we have to have it out by Monday. *[pauses]* I know He hasn't been dead for 24 hours yet. But we have an obligation to the citizens of the empire. This is big news.

Famous Last Words

[pauses] I've been thinking about that something to put a spin on the whole story, maybe reveal a side of Jesus unseen until now . . . *[snaps]* I've got it. Jesus' final words. Final words say a lot about a man. Perhaps there is something in the final words of Jesus that will put everything in perspective. . . . *[pauses]* "It is finished." *[pauses for his reaction]* That's it? Those were His final words? *[pauses for his response]* What do you mean, you haven't a clue what He meant? There could be a lot hidden in that phrase. Was it His life that was finished? Or His work? *[pauses]* Whatever it was Jesus finished on that cross, I want it tagged onto the end of that Newsreel and out to all the provinces of Rome by Monday.

[MARCUS exits. ESTHER enters. She is seated in a chair or rocker.]

ESTHER: Finished? It is finished? I have no idea what that could mean. But whatever He meant, I think I know how it began. It happened right here, in our little inn. My husband Isaiah's grandfather established the place, and it has been passed down through the years, to my father-in-law, then to us. My son now manages the inn since the death of my dear Isaiah, God rest his soul. No one was more surprised than we were by what transpired that night. After all, Bethlehem's nothing more than a pit stop on the way to Jerusalem, and I do mean pit. Nobody comes to Bethlehem. There are no sights, no tourist attractions, nothing to see, with the possible exception of the plot of ground where King David's boyhood home used to be until the Babylonians torched it. So we were scraping along, you know, lodging out a room or two a night to travelers passing through. And then one day, Caesar Augustus issues a decree that all the Roman world should be counted. Well, Isaiah gets so excited, he starts bouncing off the walls. I say, "Isaiah, what gives?" He says, "Honey, it's a census. Everyone has to go to the town of their birth." I say, "But no one lives here." He says, "Exactly. They all moved away. They have no relatives to stay with. They will all need rooms!" So we get the whole inn cleaned up, and right on schedule, grumpy travelers lined up at our door. I'm not kidding, we were wall to wall with people, and no one was pleased to be back in Bethlehem. But we just smiled and assigned the rooms until we, like every other hotel in town, were full. Now, I can't remember exactly when or how it happened, but this man, Jesus' father, he came into the inn and pleaded with Isaiah to rent him a room. He explained that his wife was pregnant and really needed a soft place to rest that night. Of course, Isaiah refused. As far as he was concerned, the place was packed, and no one else was getting a room. But he did offer the man and his wife the stable out back, which they took. Well, I was horrified. Having been through eight pregnancies myself, I know a stable is no place for a woman in that condition. When I found out that Isaiah had stuck that poor girl in the filthy stable, I nearly killed him. I decided the best thing was to give the young couple my and Isaiah's room and make my genius of a husband sleep with the animals. But by then, Mary—that was her name—was in labor. And she delivered her child right there amid the animals and filth. He was precious, that child. Just darling. You could tell by looking at Him there were great things in His future. But just in case you didn't get the idea looking at Him, the Lord sent several signs. A group of out-of-breath shepherds showed up out of the blue, claiming that angels had sung to them about the birth of the Messiah.

[ESTHER exits. ZECHARIAS enters.]

ZECHARIAS: Yes, I remember Jesus all too well. And whatever He *finished* on that cross, well, I for one am glad it's over. What happened to Him was for the good of all Israel. Caiaphas even prophesied that one man would die for the good of the people, and it has come to pass. If we hadn't squelched His fire, He would have drawn the attention of Rome, bringing more bloodshed and violence upon us. As if we haven't suffered enough! You know, I saw it coming years ago. I was just a student at the time, serving in the temple in Jerusalem and studying under the priests. He had come with His family for the Passover. This was probably 20 or so years ago, so He would have been around the age of 12. The feast had ended, and all the Jews who had come to Jerusalem for the feast were on their way home. Except the boy Jesus. He slipped away from His parents and returned to the temple courts, where He found my master, Gamaliel, and began to question him on matters of the law. He questioned Gamaliel and the other teachers on the nature of sin, the law of Moses, and many more issues too vast and deep for a boy of 12 to understand. My teacher and his colleagues were baffled by His questions. What's more, when the teachers were stumped, the boy would answer. All of the priests were amazed by His knowledge. Here before them was the poor child of a carpenter, barely 12 years old and yet with knowledge that surpassed that of men five times His age who had spent their entire lives in study of the Scriptures. I remember my fellow student Saul laughing at the sight, seeing a small child bewilder and perplex the renowned leaders of the faith. Jesus remained in the temple three days, discussing matters of the Lord with the priests. When His parents found Him, He had the nerve to chastise them for being concerned. "Didn't you know I would be in my Father's house?" Saul thought it was cute how that little boy had stumped our teacher, but I believed the boy was possessed by an evil spirit. Such a fantastic claim, that God was His Father, was nothing less than blasphemy. Whatever He was, the Lord has dealt with Him according to His deeds and words.

[ZECHARIAS exits. DANIEL enters.]

DANIEL: "It is finished?" Well, I really don't know that I'm going to be able to help you with that question. I only met Jesus one time, but He left an impression on me that day. I almost missed it too. You see, I really had no interest in going to hear some Galilean preach, but it came down to a choice: either help Mom spread manure to fertilize the garden or go listen to Jesus. Which option would you have chosen? Anyway, I started out bright and early walking toward Bethsaida. I hadn't gone a block when Mom came running after me with a basket of lunch: some bread and couple of fish. That basket of food is the reason I had the opportunity to meet Jesus. You see, there were TONS of people who came out to hear Jesus preach. TONS! Somebody said there were 5,000 men there, but if you count the wives and children, there had to be four or five times that many total. Jesus preached until the late afternoon, and then all of a sudden, He stopped. From where I was seated, I could see Him talking to His friends. I figured they were going to send everyone off to get dinner, so I found a nice spot to sit down and eat. Before I could, one of Jesus' friends came running to me. He introduced himself as Andrew and asked if I minded bringing my lunch to Jesus. Like I'm going to turn down the chance to meet a celebrity. So we ran up the hill, and Andrew introduced me and gave my lunch to Jesus. Jesus said a prayer and then began to break the bread. Like I said, I only had five loaves of bread and two small fish. But in Jesus' hands, the food multiplied. He filled basket after basket with bread and fish. His friends and followers passed the baskets among the crowd, and everyone ate. Some even had seconds! By the time it was all over, my tiny lunch had fed all those thousands of people. And to top it off, there were 12 baskets FULL of leftovers. I don't know what He meant when He said, "It is finished." But one thing I do know—that guy knew how to finish BIG!

[DANIEL exits. JUNA enters.]

JUNA: You know, I've had so many people coming and asking me about Jesus. Ever since He came to see me two years ago, everywhere I go people wanna know about Jesus. *[shrugs]* All I know is that one minute my daddy is kissing me good-bye, saying he's going to find a miracle man, and the next minute, poof! There was Jesus in my room! This all happened about two years ago when I got sick. Really sick. I mean really, really, REALLY sick. I didn't feel like eating, or playing, or nothing. All I did was lay around and moan like this. *[she moans, melodramatically as only a little girl can do]* Anyway, my daddy brought in all kinds of doctors to look at me, and none of them knew what was wrong or how to fix it. My parents prayed night and day for an answer, and one day, my daddy overheard about this guy named Jesus. Jesus was going all over the place healing sick people and blind people, and my daddy figured maybe Jesus could heal me too. He told my mommy and me about it, and Mommy thought it was a good idea. So Daddy kissed me good-bye and set off with his servants. After that, I rolled over and went to sleep. . . . And then the next thing I know, I feel this warm hand in mine and hear a voice say, "Little girl, get up!" I shot straight up and replied, "I'm not a little girl. I'm a big girl." Well all of a sudden, my parents start hugging me and kissing me and screaming, "She's alive! She's alive!" My parents thanked Him and thanked Him for what He had done. Finally I just shouted, "Hey! What's going on?" And that's when they told me. After my daddy left and I fell asleep, the doctors examined me and told my mommy that I had DIED! Everybody in the house started crying. They sent a servant after my daddy to tell him the news and that they didn't need to bother Jesus anymore. By the time he found my daddy, my daddy was on his way back with Jesus. Daddy was very upset, as you can imagine, but Jesus told him, "She's not dead! She's just sleeping." He came home with my dad, and when He got here, He came into my room and woke me. I don't know if I was dead or just sleeping, but I guess if I had been dead, I probably wouldn't remember, huh? *[thoughtful pause]* You know what I don't understand? If He is the Son of God, how could He be dead? Can you really kill God? I don't think so! He promised me that one day we'd spend more time together. He'd come and take me to His home in Heaven. *[pause]* God always keeps His promises. Doesn't He?

[JUNA exits. BARRABAS enters.]

BARABBAS: I suppose I was one of the last people to have a close encounter with Jesus—unless you count the men who drove the nails into His wrists. They should have been my wrists, in the eyes of Rome. But due to some politicking between Pilate and the High Council, I was released and Jesus sent to His death. They threw Him in a holding cell just before the circus on Pilate's balcony. He was a mess—I mean beaten, bloodied, lucky to be alive. The soldiers had really messed Him over. They gave Him the kind of treatment usually reserved for enemies of the state like me. He didn't belong there. I could tell just by looking at Him that He was no criminal. That made it all the more incredible when I saw that He never spoke a word in His defense. He went where He was led without a complaint, without an argument. "Aren't You the one who claimed to be the king of the Jews?" they asked Him. "Are you the Messiah, the man who will deliver Israel from its chains?" He looked at them with weary eyes and spoke with absolute peace. "You are correct in saying that I am." The Roman guards led us to the balcony of Pilate's home. There, the people of Jerusalem demanded my release and Jesus' death. Ironically, the crime the Jews accused Him of was the same crime that had imprisoned me—attempting to incite a rebellion. Why was He killed? *[shrugs]* Who am I to argue? He took my place on the cross and died in my place. I heard about His final moments, asking for a drink and receiving a vinegar-soaked sponge. Then He gasped, "It is finished," dropped His head, and died. I don't know what He meant. But I do wish I could have one more chance to talk to Him. I want to know why He would choose to die in my place, when we both knew He had done nothing wrong.

[BARABBAS exits. MARCUS reenters, on his cell phone.]

MARCUS: So that's it, huh? A baby is born in a stable, grows up to be a miracle worker, makes a lot of people happy, makes a few people mad, raises the dead, dies a martyr. "It is finished. . . ." Well, I don't know what I was expecting. Something better than that. I mean, to have Him dead and buried after all those miracles seems—I don't know—anticlimactic. . . . Well, not that I put any stock in the Hebrew mythology of the Messiah who will come to deliver them, but I almost get the feeling that the story isn't quite over. . . . Maybe, maybe this miracle man has one more miracle. . . .

[MARY MAGDALENE enters again.]

MARCUS: Perhaps we'll never know what Jesus meant when He said, "It is finished." Then again, the answer might be right under our noses. Good-bye, Harry.

[MARCUS exits. MARY kneels, crying.]

MARY: They've taken His body. How could they do this? Haven't we suffered enough? They've killed my Savior, and now . . . they've taken all that was left away from me.

[JESUS approaches MARY from stage right.]

JESUS: Woman, why are you crying?
MARY: They have taken my Lord away, and I don't know where they have put Him.
JESUS: Who is it you are looking for?

MARY: *[turns to look at JESUS]* Sir, if You have carried Him away, tell me where You have put Him, and I will get Him.

JESUS: Mary.

MARY: *[falls at Jesus' feet, recognizing Him]* You're alive.

JESUS: Do not hold onto me, but go and tell my disciples and Peter that I have risen just as I said.

Mother's Day Mayhem

Brett Parker

Summary: A teenage girl comes home to find that she's forgotten that it's Mother's Day. She goes crazy thinking she doesn't have anything to give to her mom.
Characters:
DEBBIE—a young, energetic girl, around 10 or 12 years old
MOM—calm, loving mother of DEBBIE
Setting: the living room of DEBBIE'S home
Props: couch, coffee table, newspaper, book bag, pencil, notepad, plastic telephone, and a piggy bank with change

The living room is set as DEBBIE enters.

DEBBIE: *[walks in, drops book bag and sits on couch in front of coffee table]* What a day! School is so tough. Oh well, at least tomorrow is Friday. And that means the weekend is almost here! *[stands up and does a celebration dance]* What am I going to do this weekend? Hmm . . . maybe I can go shopping at the mall! Or I bet there's a new movie coming out at the movie theater! *[picks up a newspaper on coffee table]* What?! Oh no! This Sunday is Mother's Day?! Oh great! I didn't get anything for Mom! OK, let's not panic. *[to herself]* All right, Debbie, you have to think. I know! *[runs offstage, comes back on with a piggy bank]* I'll buy her a present! *[She opens the piggy bank and pours change onto coffee table. She then counts the money.]* Fifty-eight cents! It's perfect! Now let's see . . . what does Mom like? *[thinks]* Chocolate! *[reaches for phone on coffee table, dials a number]* Hello? How much chocolate can I get with 58 cents? One *box*?! Great! I'll take—huh? Oh, just one *chocolate*? No thanks, never mind. *[hangs up phone]* Well, I guess I can't buy her a gift. What could I do? Mother's Day is only three days away! *[pauses]* Wait! *[jumps up]* I'll build her something. That's it! But what? *[thinks aloud]* A towel rack? No no, too boring. A makeup cabinet? Nope, that wouldn't work. A birdhouse?! Yes, she would love that! That's what I'll do! OK, so what do I need. I need to make a list. *[grabs a notepad and a pencil out of book bag]* I need some wood, a saw, some nails, *[starts to doubt]* . . . a hammer . . . Oh, this will never work! Where am I going to get all of this stuff? How am I going to build a birdhouse? I have trouble making things with building blocks! Mom is going to be so disappointed in me. *[sits on couch and buries her face in her hands]*
MOM: *[walks into living room]* Hey, Debbie! You're home from school! Debbie—what's wrong, hon? Why do you look so sad?
DEBBIE: I wanted to get you something for Mother's Day, but I waited until

it was too late. Now I don't have enough time to buy you anything. And I certainly can't make you anything! I know that you're disappointed in me. I'm sorry, Mom.

MOM: Oh, Debbie, I'm not disappointed in you. *[puts arm around DEBBIE]* You don't need to give me any gifts for me to be happy with you. I love you, and the best thing you could give me for Mother's Day is to simply spend time with me.

DEBBIE: That's it? But don't you like getting presents, Mom?

MOM: Well, of course, I like getting presents. But what's important to moms on Mother's Day is that they know that their children love them and that they want to try their hardest to be good kids. And that's exactly what you're doing.

DEBBIE: Really? I never thought about it like that! *[thinks for a moment]* But, Mom, I still want to do something for you on your special day. What can I do?

MOM: Well, let's see . . . how about breakfast in bed?

DEBBIE: I can do that!!

MOM: Good! Then why don't you just do that for my present?

DEBBIE: Oh, you just wait, Mom! This is going to be the best breakfast you've ever had! I'm talking everything you can imagine!

MOM: *[laughs]* Don't get too ahead of yourself now. Remember that we still have to get up and go to church on Sunday. *[starts to exit]*

DEBBIE: *[gets up to follow her]* Yeah, yeah. But you're going to love this! You like eggs, Mom? Fried? Scrambled? Over easy? How 'bout toast? French toast? Cinnamon toast? Cheese toast? You're going to need jelly with all that toast! Grape? Strawberry? Apple? This is going to be the best Mother's Day ever! *[continues talking as she exits]*

The Heart of the Matter

Susan Sundwall

Characters:
ANNIE—teenage girl
CHUCK—teenage boy, brother of ANNIE
MARCUS—teenage boy, friend of CHUCK
MOM—mother of ANNIE and CHUCK, sweet middle-aged woman
Setting: living room
Props: chair, plate of oatmeal cookies, comic book
Costumes: modern-day clothing, age appropriate for each character

ANNIE: *[enters stage left waving her hands]* Oh no! Oh no!

CHUCK: *[looks up]* Hey, what's up, sis?

ANNIE: I lost it, that's what!

CHUCK: *[stands up, looks around]* Uh, Annie? What's the *it* you lost?

ANNIE: The whole thing! I lost the whole thing!

CHUCK: Well, let me help you find IT.

ANNIE: *[looks frantic]* I'll need to retrace my steps. OK, I had it yesterday . . . and I didn't want Mom to see it, so I—

CHUCK: Did you hide IT in your bedroom or your backpack? Do I get any clues?

ANNIE: You're not being very helpful!

MARCUS: *[enters stage right]* Chuck! Annie! What's up, gang?

ANNIE: Oh! Marcus! Maybe you can help too.

MARCUS: Sure.

ANNIE: I can't find the Mother's Day gift I bought for Mom.

CHUCK: *[turns to the audience and points to himself]* Why didn't she tell ME that?

MOM: *[enters stage left carrying a plate of cookies]* Anybody hungry?

MARCUS: *[rubs his hands together]* Wow! Cookies!

CHUCK: Oatmeal, my favorite!

ANNIE: *[throws her hands up]* This is NO time for eating.

MOM: Goodness, Annie, I'll bet your brother and Marcus don't think so. *[offers them the cookies]* Dig in!

CHUCK & MARCUS: *[each one takes one]* Thanks!

ANNIE: *[rolls her eyes]* Very bad timing, Mom. *[puts her hands on her hips]*

MOM: *[shrugs and looks puzzled]* I'll get some milk *[exits stage right with cookies]*

MARCUS: Boy, I wish my Mom made cookies like these!

ANNIE: I suppose you'll be too busy chomping away to help me now!

CHUCK: What did you get for Mom anyway?

ANNIE: A really nice heart-shaped pillow that says I Love You.

MARCUS: You could have fooled me.

ANNIE: What?

MARCUS: It didn't exactly sound like you love your mom.

CHUCK: Marcus is right. You were pretty harsh. All she did was bring us cookies. It's not her fault you lost the gift.

ANNIE: *[raises her hands in frustration]* Tomorrow's Mother's Day! I spent my whole allowance, and if I don't find that card and pillow, I won't have a thing to give her.

CHUCK: Hmm . . . I wonder if that's a good excuse for being rude. What do you think, Marcus?

MARCUS: *[holds half-eaten cookie up and admires it]* I wouldn't be rude to anyone who makes cookies like these!

ANNIE: *[with hands on her hips]* All I said was . . .

CHUCK: *[imitates ANNIE throwing his hands up]* This is *no* time for eating!

MARCUS: *[imitates ANNIE with hands on his hips]* Very bad timing, Mom!

ANNIE: I did not look like . . . *[drops her hands to her side, looks self-conscious]* Oh.

CHUCK: *[puts his hand on her shoulder]* You can ACT like you love her, you know. Just use what you feel in your own heart. That would be a great gift.

MARCUS: Even better than a heart pillow.

ANNIE: I didn't mean to be rude. I guess I'm mad at myself for losing her gift.

CHUCK: We'll keep looking.

ANNIE: *[her shoulders slump a little]* Thanks, guys. Ugh, poor Mom. Man, sometimes I'm a real moron, huh?

MARCUS: *[grinning]* You sure are! But if you're extra nice, maybe she'll teach you how to make oatmeal cookies!

ANNIE: *[punches MARCUS lightly on the arm]* OK, we can look again in a few minutes. I want to do something first. *[calls as she exits stage right]* Mom, need some help?

Proverbs 31 Mommy

by Brett Parker

Thank you so much, Mommy,
For all the wonderful things you do.
God knew what He was doing
When He gave me a mommy like you.

Before I even wake up,
You are busy in the dark.
And on days when the sun is shining,
You take me to the park.

At nighttime when I've brushed my teeth,
You tuck me into bed.
You read to me the Bible
And all the things that Jesus said.

You pick up my toys when I forget
And make my lunches too.
I am certain there is nothing
That my mommy cannot do.

You love me when I'm happy;
You love me when I'm sad.
You care for me when I scrape
    my knee
And when I'm feeling bad.

You teach me how to be like Jesus,
That He is the greatest reward.
You make me and Daddy proud
Because of your love for the Lord.

Thank you so much, Mommy,
For all the wonderful things you do.
God knew what He was doing
When He gave me a mommy like you.

Just How Blessed
Dixie Phillips

Just how blessed can one child be?
To have a mommy who prays for me!

A Mother's Role
Dolores Steger

A mother, in life, may play many roles—
Ones she doesn't even rehearse.
At times she's a teacher, a model of faith,
A leader, a mentor, a nurse.

But her leading role, for days upon days,
Is obvious, yes, it's true.
The role that she plays shows so wonderfully well
Her abiding love for you.

Dad's Cooking
Dixie Phillips

Child enters with antacids but doesn't show them until his last line.

We keep our moms so busy from morning until night.
Taking care of all of us requires all their might!
So to honor my mom, I came up here to say,
"Here are some antacids, Mom; Dad's cooking today!"

My Mommy Has a Mommy
Dixie Phillips

My mommy has a mommy who is here today.
And I just want to honor her and stand up here and say,
"Thank you, Grandma, for loving me.
And thank you too for a great family."

Drama Queen
Dixie Phillips

My mom calls me her drama queen.
I love to act, and I love to sing.
I love fancy costumes I sometimes wear.
I adore the way my mom fixes my hair.
But there is no acting today when I say,
"My mom's the best! Happy Mother's Day!"

Firstborn
Dixie Phillips

I'm the firstborn of our family.
But most of the time no one listens to me.
I have such great advice to give to my brother.
He always reminds me, "You're not my mother!"
But today while I have your utmost attention,
Something very important I'd like to mention:
I thank God for the mother He gave to me.
I'm proud to be under a branch on her family tree.

Night Duty
Ruth Powell

"Mama, bring some water,"
My little daughter said.
With sleepy head and tired feet
I stumbled from my bed.

I filled a glass and stopped
To get an extra blanket;
But she was fast asleep again,
So I stood there and drank it.

Mommy's Boy

Dixie Phillips

I'm my mommy's pride and joy.
Besides my dad, I'm her favorite boy!

And my sisters can't be beat.
They act like Mommy, 'cept not as sweet.

How did my mommy get such a clan?
She married my daddy. It was all in God's plan.

Smart Mom

Dixie Phillips

Daddy says the day my mom married my dad
Was proof to him of what a smart mom I had.

Just how smart is she, you say?
Well, she's the one who taught me to pray.

She taught me how to talk to God.
And I was just a girl of seven.

Thank you, Mommy, for teaching me to pray.
And thank you, Mommy, for leading me the right way!

Cultured

Dixie Phillips

I've got an East Coast mother and a West Coast dad.
We've got more culture than most folks have had.

But the greatest gift my parents gave to me
Was a godly home where my young eyes could see:

Mother loves my father and Father loves my mother.
That love is contagious and then we all love each other.

I asked my mother one day while eating dinner.
"How'd we get this love to make our family such a winner?"

Without batting an eye, she said it came from God above.
He created families, and He fills each home with love.

No Mommy Like Mine

Dixie Phillips

There's no mommy like my mommy, and that's no lie.
If you listen for a minute, I will tell you why.

My mom never thinks of herself—not one bit.
And if I rip my pants, she has a nifty sewing kit.

You can always find her in the kitchen cooking.
And daddy says there's not one woman better looking.

So I just have to bow my head to God and pray,
"Thank You, dear Lord, for my mommy this Mother's Day."

All Tied Up

Susan Sundwall

Characters:
ANNIE—teenage girl
CHUCK—teenage boy, brother of ANNIE
CARLA—teenage girl, cousin of ANNIE and CHUCK
DAD—father of ANNIE and CHUCK
Setting: mall
Props: 3 shopping bags, 3 neckties (1 purple tie for CARLA's bag, 2 identical yellow ties for CHUCK's and ANNIE's bags)

CHUCK: Boy, Dad is gonna love this!
ANNIE: *[runs in from stage left carrying shopping bag]* Oh boy!
CARLA: *[runs in behind ANNIE carrying shopping bag]* Wait up!
CHUCK: *[looks up]* Hey, I didn't know you two were in the mall.
ANNIE: Aunt Nora drove us here.
CARLA: Yeah, Mom, Annie, and I just bought Father's Day presents.
CHUCK: Ha! I'll bet mine's better than either of yours.
ANNIE: Oh yeah? So let's see it!
CHUCK: Oh no. Let's see yours first.
CARLA: *[pulls the purple tie out of her bag]* Here's mine!
CHUCK: Ewww.
ANNIE: It's not SO bad.
CARLA: Well, my dad loves purple! He has a red shirt to go with it.
CHUCK: C'mon Annie, what did ya get?
ANNIE: Something he'll use over and over.
CHUCK: Like those lime green sunglasses you got him last year?
ANNIE: Hey! He wore those . . . once.
CARLA: Did he have an orange shirt to go with them?

[DAD walks in quietly stage right and stands back, watching them.]

ANNIE: *[looks bug-eyed at CARLA]* You saw it? Well, guess who gave it to him? *[jerks her thumb at CHUCK]*
CARLA: *[sees DAD and makes small signaling motions to CHUCK and ANNIE]* Uh . . . guys? Um . . .
CHUCK: *[ignores her]* Dad is a cool guy. He kinda liked that shirt. *[He makes a quick grab for ANNIE'S bag.]* So what's in the bag, supershopper?
ANNIE: *[pulls away]* None of your . . .

[DAD walks over and stands behind them. ANNIE and CHUCK start a tug of war with the bags, then sense DAD's presence and freeze.]

CHUCK: *[looks up]* Dad!

ANNIE: *[looks up]* Dad!

CARLA: Uh-oh. *[puts her hands up, palms out]* I tried to warn you!

DAD: I sure hope those bags are sturdy. I'm here to take you both home— ready to go?

CHUCK: *[sneers at ANNIE]* Uh, I guess.

ANNIE: *[puts her bag behind her back and makes a face at CHUCK]* Sure.

DAD: *[looks thoughtful]* You know, while I was getting the car, I thought of the time my brother and I gave our dad the best Father's Day present ever.

ANNIE: Really?

CHUCK: Something way expensive, huh, Dad?

DAD: The day before Father's Day, my brother, Carla's dad *[smiles at CARLA],* and I had a huge fight over a bag of popcorn.

ANNIE: I'll bet it was his fault too, huh, Dad?

CHUCK: *[scowls at ANNIE]* Popcorn fights are the best! Who won, Dad?

DAD: Nobody ever wins in a popcorn fight, Chuck. But our dad came in and surprised us.

ANNIE: Ewww . . . like you did just now?

CHUCK: Did you get clobbered?

DAD: *[smiles]* No, he surprised us by saying that the best Father's Day present we could ever give him was to just get along *[puts a hand on each of their shoulders]*.

CHUCK: You know, if I had a brother instead of a sister . . .

ANNIE: *[makes a sour face]* Lime green sunglasses would have been a lot easier.

DAD: *[laughs]* It was tough all right. But we gave it a shot just for Dad, and it wasn't so bad. We even cleaned up the popcorn.

CARLA: I'll have to ask him about that.

DAD: I'm sure he'll remember. I'll be in the car. *[exits stage right]*

ANNIE: I guess we could *try* to get along better, just for Dad.

CHUCK: Yeah, I guess.

[They each look into their bags.]

ANNIE: So what did ya get him?

CHUCK: *[pulls out a yellow tie]* Think he'll like it?

ANNIE: *[pulls out a yellow tie]* Yeah, I do.

CARLA: Well, maybe he'll spill ketchup on one and need a spare!

[They exit laughing and playing with the ties.]

Something Good
Dolores Steger

When something good happens,
I know it to be
A blessing the dear Lord
Has sent right to me.

And the very best blessing
That I've ever had
Is the gift, and the love,
And the care of my dad.

We Honor Fathers
Dolores Steger

We honor fathers here today.
They stand so strong and tall.
And as we do, we honor God—
The Father of us all.

Fathers to All
Dolores Steger

A grandpa, an uncle, a brother, a son—
They can be fathers to those who have none.

A nephew, a neighbor, a really close friend,
May serve as fathers for disheartened men.

Men the world over may answer God's call
To help those in need and be fathers to all.

Give Thanks for Fathers
Dolores Steger

Give thanks for fathers, their patience, their care,
Their guidance, assurance, just knowing they're there.

Give thanks for fathers; the families they lead
Rely on them for all the things that they need.

Give thanks for fathers, their love extends far.
Give thanks for fathers, a blessing they are.

Training
Dolores Steger

My dad's in training constantly.
He works at it so purposely.
He perseveres. Why? Now I see—
To lift another weight from me.

A Father and His Child
Dolores Steger

Paste and tape are very good
At making most things stick.
And superglue can bind them fast—
I mean real ultraquick.

But I've told Dad so often,
And watched him as he smiled:
There's nothing like the bond between
A father and his child.